"This Land Is Your Land"
Let's Explore the Heartland

Jill C. Wheeler

Published by Abdo & Daughters, 4940 Viking Drive, Suite 622, Edina, MN 55435.

Library bound edition distributed by Rockbottom Books, Pentagon Tower, P.O. Box 36036, Minneapolis, Minnesota 55435.

ISBN: 1-56239-297-2

Inside Photos by:
Bettmann Archives: 5, 6, 7, 8, 9, 11, 14, 15, 16, 17, 18, 19, 24
Archive Photos: 4
Wide World Photos: 20, 22, 23
John Hamilton: 2, 10, 12, 13, 14, 15

Edited by John Hamilton

Library of Congress Cataloging–in–Publication Data
Wheeler, Jill C., 1964-
    The Midwest and the heartland / Jill C. Wheeler
        p.   cm — (America, this land is your land)
    Includes bibliographical references (p.) and index.
    ISBN 1-56239-297-2
    1. Middle West -- Juvenile literature. [1. Middle West .]
  I. Title. II. Series: Wheeler, Jill C., 1964- America, this land
is your land.
F351.W55   1994
956—dc20   94-10647
                                            CIP
                                            AC

Contents

◀ *A rainbow shines down on the Heartland.*

Let's Explore the Heartland

The Midwest and the Heartland are a beautiful, diverse region. Industrial cities sit next to gently rolling farmlands. Mighty rivers and majestic lakes cross the land.

Years ago, this area was a wilderness of forests and prairies. Many tribes of Native Americans lived here. Wild animals and birds thrived. Fish filled the lakes and streams. The rich landscape attracted many early settlers. The settlers wanted to grow crops.

Agriculture is still important in the Midwest. This is the bread basket of the United States. Farmers here grow more food than any other area. Fields of corn, oats, hay, and soybeans dot the landscape. Farmers use some of this grain to feed cattle and hogs. These animals produce meat.

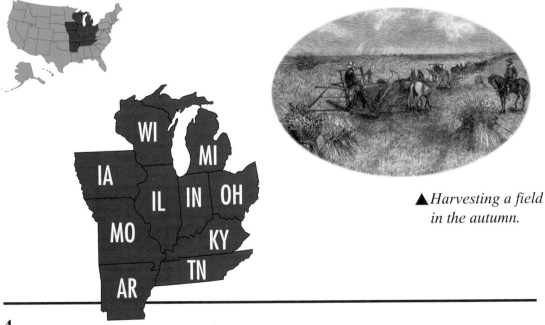

▲Harvesting a field in the autumn.

Wild weather like blizzards and tornadoes often hit the Midwest.

The Midwest is not all farms. It has many major cities, too. People around the world know Detroit makes cars. Chicago is a financial and communications center. Farther south, Nashville is the capital of country music. St. Louis is an industrial and cultural center.

Midwesterners enjoy a varied climate. The change of seasons brings big differences in temperatures. In the north, winters can be long and cold. Summers can be hot and humid. In the southern Midwest, winters are shorter and milder. Summers are even hotter than up north. This *continental* *climate* occurs only in the middle of large land areas.

This climate helps farmers grow crops. The warm summer sun and rains help plants grow quickly.

Sometimes, the Midwest has violent weather. Thunderstorms can bring hail and strong winds. Some create tornadoes. In the winter, blizzards bring heavy snows and wind to the North.

Some people think the Midwest is all flatland and farms. In the next chapters, we'll see that the Midwest is much more.

Historical Highlights

Midwestern history is a story of explorers and Native Americans. It is a story of fierce battles for land and brave pioneers. Later, it became a story of inventors and industry. Let's look at how the Midwest and Heartland grew:

▲ *Daniel Boone leads settlers through the Kentucky wilderness.*

1541 Spanish explorer Hernando de Soto spends the winter in the Midwest. He is at a Native American village in Arkansas.

1668 Frenchman Father Jacques Marquette founds the first Midwest settlement. He calls it Saulte Saint Marie. It is in Michigan.

1673 Marquette and explorer Louis Joliet travel down the Mississippi River. They are looking for a water route to Asia.

1682 French explorer Robert Cavelier claims the Mississippi Valley for France. He names the country Louisiana.

1701 Frenchman Antoine Cadillac founds a city. He calls it Detroit.

1731 French settlers found the first permanent settlement. It is Vincennes, Indiana.

1763 Native American Chief Pontiac lays siege to Detroit. The battle lasts 175 days.

1764 Auguste Chouteau founds a city. He calls it St. Louis.

1767 Daniel Boone begins exploring Kentucky.

1775–1783 Settlers and Native Americans fight in Kentucky for control of the land.

1776 Native Americans attack the Boonesborough settlement in Kentucky. They capture Daniel Boone's daughter. He rescues her.

1795 Settlers and Native Americans sign a treaty in Ohio. It is the Treaty of Greenville. It ends the fighting between them.

1800 Spain gives Iowa and Louisiana to France.

1803 The *Louisiana Purchase* expands the United States.

1804 The Lewis and Clark expedition leaves St. Louis. The expedition is going to explore the Louisiana Purchase. Explorer Sergeant Floyd dies near Sioux City, Iowa. He is the only member of the expedition to die on the journey.

1811 An earthquake shakes the Mississippi Valley. It is the strongest ever to hit the continent.

1811 William Henry Harrison defeats a Native American uprising. This is the Battle of Tippecanoe. People fight the battle in Indiana.

1818 Illinois becomes the 21st state.

◄*Life along the Erie Canal.*

▼*The great Chicago fire of 1871.*

The Indianapolis 500 roars to a start on Memorial Day, 1926. The very first Indy 500 was run in 1911.

1832 The Black Hawk War begins. Chief Black Hawk leads Fox and Sauk tribes to recapture tribal lands.

1832 Workers complete the Ohio-Erie Canal. It lets ships pass along the Great Lakes.

1836 Arkansas becomes a state.

1837 Michigan becomes the 26th state.

1840 Settlers travel the National Road. It extends from Cumberland, Maryland, to Vandalia, Illinois.

1846 Iowa becomes the first free state in the old Louisiana Territory.

1848 Wisconsin becomes the 30th state.

1849 Fort Smith, Arkansas, becomes a thriving frontier outpost. Gold-seekers on their way west get supplies here.

1855 Prospectors begin mining iron ore in Michigan.

1855 The first Soo Canal opens. The canal lets ships travel from Lake Superior to Lake Michigan and Lake Erie. The ships carry iron ore from the shores of Lake Superior. Workers use the ore to make steel.

1858 Abraham Lincoln and Stephen Douglas debate. Each is trying to win the presidency. The debates help people learn about Lincoln.

1862 Congress passes the *Homestead Act*. The Act offers free land to settlers.

Abraham Lincoln debates Stephen Douglas in 1858.

◄ Four students were killed by National Guard troops during anti-war riots at Kent State University, Ohio, in 1970.

1867 The first railroad runs across Iowa. It goes from the Mississippi to Council Bluffs.

1868 Voters elect Ulysses S. Grant president. He is from Illinois.

1870 John D. Rockefeller founds the Standard Oil Company. It begins in Cleveland, Ohio.

1870 Benjamin Goodrich opens a factory in Akron, Ohio. The factory makes rubber products.

1871 Fire sweeps Chicago. The flames destroy much of the city.

1875 Horses run the first Kentucky Derby.

1878 More than 5,000 people die from *cholera* and *yellow fever* in Memphis, Tennessee.

1887 Prospectors find large deposits of *bauxite* in Arkansas. Metal workers use bauxite to make aluminium.

1906 Prospectors discover the nation's only diamond mine in Arkansas.

1911 Drivers race the first Indianapolis 500.

1925 The Scopes "Monkey Trial" takes place in Tennessee. The trial debates the origins of humans.

1942 Scientists set off the first controlled nuclear chain reaction. Enrico Fermi leads the effort at the University of Chicago.

1945 Missouri native Harry S. Truman becomes president. World War II ends with Japan's surrender. Leaders sign the treaty on the battleship *U.S.S. Missouri.*

1957 Federal troops come to Little Rock, Arkansas, to enforce *desegregation* laws.

1968 The Democratic National Convention begins in Chicago. Riots break out.

1968 An *assassin* kills civil rights leader Martin Luther King, Jr., in Memphis.

1970 National guardsmen kill four students during anti-war protests. The deaths are at Kent State University in Ohio.

1977 Elvis Presley dies in Memphis, Tennessee.

1992 Voters elect Arkansas Governor Bill Clinton president.

◄ Soldiers make sure African–American students get safely to school in Little Rock, Arkansas, in 1957.

The Lay of the Land

The landscape of the Midwest and Heartland is rich in contrasts. In the East, the Central Lowlands have gently rolling farmlands. This is some of the world's best farmland. This area has a large network of roads and railways. It is easy to build on this flatland.

In the North lie the Great Lakes. These five lakes form a huge inland waterway. *Glaciers* formed the lakes thousands of years ago. Many ships still use the lakes today.

The Mississippi River runs through the center of the Midwest. Many other *tributary* rivers empty into the Mississippi River. The Mississippi River and its tributaries form one of the world's largest river systems.

A weather vane from a barn in central Iowa. The Midwest, with its rich soil, is home to some of the world's best farmland. ▶

These rivers helped settlers travel through the Midwest. Many settlers made their homes near the rivers. Businesses in these towns grew as well. The businesses could transport the products they made on the river. Many of these river towns still thrive.

In the southern part of the Midwest, we find the Interior Highlands. The Highlands have wooded hills and low mountains. This beautiful land attracts many tourists. Residents harvest timber from the hills.

▲ *The Mississippi River flowed well over its banks during the floods of 1993. In some cases, entire towns found themselves underwater.*

The Midwest and Heartland have many special attractions, too:

Mammoth Cave in Kentucky has giant *stalactites* and *stalagmites*. It has more than 150 miles of passageways on five levels. A hunter discovered the cave in 1799.

Lookout Mountain in Tennessee is 2,146 feet above sea level. On a clear day, visitors at the top can see

◀ Cliffs along Lake Superior.

five states. Civil War soldiers fought a battle on the mountain in 1863.

Hot Springs, Arkansas, has become a well-known resort. The waters in these springs are naturally hot. They can reach 143 degrees Fahrenheit. The springs are in the Ouachita Mountains.

The Great Lakes feature rocky cliffs and scenic waterfalls. They are Lake Superior, Lake Huron, Lake Erie, Lake Ontario, and Lake Michigan. Their shores are home to many great parks. One is Pictured Rocks National Lakeshore. This park features castle-like rock formations.

The Bluegrass Region of Kentucky and Ohio is well named. Lush grass has blue-gray blossoms each spring. This grass grows naturally only in Kentucky. The area is famous for racehorses and tobacco.

Indiana Dunes National Lakeshore has dunes up to 10,000 years old. Wind and water push the dunes farther back each year. Young dunes have no plants and animals. Soil covers the older dunes. They are home to many plants and animals.

▼ Harvesting bales of hay in an Iowa farm field.

Plants & Animals

Years ago, the Midwest and Heartland teemed with plants and animals. Native Americans hunted deer, quail, and buffalo. They ate berries and wild rice. They fished for trout and walleye.

This food attracted early Europeans. Trappers also came to the Heartland. The trappers sold the furs they collected. Beaver and fox *pelts* were very popular.

▲ *Black bear are more common in the northern parts of the Midwest.*

▼ *A flock of Canada geese take to the air.*

Humans have reduced the wildlife population today. Yet the Midwest is still a favorite place for hunters and fishers. Deer are plentiful. So are game birds such as pheasants, ruffed grouse, and Canada geese. Lakes and streams have many fish. These include bass, perch, and pike.

Many common animals live in the Midwest. They include raccoons, squirrels, skunks, and badgers. Black bears and coyotes live in the northern Midwest. Oppossums and chipmunks are common, too.

In the air, look and listen for mockingbirds, bluebirds, and bright red cardinals. You may also see an American bald eagle. Other birds here are sandhill cranes, woodpeckers, hawks, and Cape May warblers. Many of these birds spend their summers in the north. They fly south for the winter.

▲ *A chipmunk.*

The lakeshore dunes feature a unique collection of plants. These include beachgrass, sandy cherry, and cottonwood trees. Beech trees are common here, too. Forests in the Midwest may be hardwoods, such as maple. They may also be pine forests, such as white pine. Other forests have both hardwoods and pine trees.

The Midwest features tasty fruits, too. Blueberries, raspberries, and huckleberries grow wild. Some areas are famous for grapes. People use the grapes to make wine.

It's no wonder the Heartland attracted early settlers. The next chapter looks at some of the people who called this land home.

◀ *Deer are plentiful in the Midwest.*

Famous Folks

Douglas MacArthur (1880–1964) General MacArthur was born in Little Rock, Arkansas. He led United States and Allied forces in the Pacific in World War II.

Black Hawk (1767–1838) Black Hawk was chief of the Sauk and Fox tribes. He helped British soldiers in the War of 1812. Later, he fought U.S. soldiers. He did not want his people pushed farther west. He was born in Illinois.

Ernest Hemingway (1899–1961) This famous writer began his career as a newspaper reporter. Later, he joined the Red Cross and drove an ambulance during World War I. He was a native of Oak Park, Illinois.

Cole Porter (1893–1964) This songwriter was born in Peru, Indiana. He wrote the words and music for more than 30 hit songs.

Abraham Lincoln (1809–1865) Lincoln was the nation's 16th president. He was born in Hodgenville, Kentucky. His life came to a tragic end in 1865. An assassin shot him to death in Washington, D.C.

Ronald Reagan (1911–) The 40th president of the U.S. was born in Tampico, Illinois. He began his career as a sportscaster in Iowa. Then he moved to Hollywood and became an actor. He made nearly 50 movies. He was governor of California before he became president.

Thomas Alva Edison (1847–1931) This inventor was born in Milan, Ohio. He invented the light bulb and the phonograph.

Bill Clinton (1946–) U.S. President Bill Clinton was born in Hope, Arkansas. Before becoming president, he was governor of Arkansas. He also taught at a law school and worked as a lawyer.

William Frederick "Buffalo Bill" Cody (1846–1917) Cody was an Army scout and Pony Express rider. He killed nearly 5,000 buffalo in 18 months. Railroad workers used the buffalo meat for food. Cody was from Scott County, Iowa.

Muhammad Ali (1942–) Ali was born Cassius Clay in Louisville, Kentucky. Some people consider him the greatest heavyweight boxer of all time. He won the World Heavyweight title in 1964.

Henry Ford (1863–1947) Ford produced his first automobile in 1893. He founded the Ford Motor Company in 1903. Ford invented the assembly line method of making cars. He was from Dearborn, Michigan.

Will Keith Kellogg (1860–1951) Kellogg and his brother invented corn flakes. This changed the way Americans ate breakfast. He founded his own cereal company. He was born in Battle Creek, Michigan.

Josephine Baker (1906–1974) Baker was a singer and dancer from St. Louis, Missouri. She ran away  from home when she was 14. Soon after, she entered show business. She became very famous in Paris.

Dale Carnegie (1888–1935) Carnegie was born in Maryville, Missouri. He began as a traveling salesman. Later, he began teaching speechmaking. He wrote a best-selling book to help people succeed.

Walter Cronkite, Jr. (1916–) Cronkite worked for CBS News for more than 30 years. He was a prize-winning reporter and news anchor. He was born in St. Joseph, Missouri.

James Cash Penney (1875–1971) This native of Hamilton, Missouri, built a department store empire. He began his career with one store in Wyoming. He became chairman of the J.C. Penney Company.

James Butler "Wild Bill" Hickock (1837–1876) Hickock was a dashing scout and U.S. marshal. He had many escapes from danger. As a marshal in the wild west, he killed many outlaws. He was from Troy Grove, Illinois.

Scott Joplin (1868–1917) Joplin was a pianist and composer. He helped develop a style of music called Ragtime. Born in Texarkana, Arkansas, he became a professional musician while still a teenager.

George Washington Carver (1864–1943) Carver was a scientist and teacher. He created products from peanuts  and sweet potatoes. He was born in Diamond Grove, Missouri.

Clark Gable (1901–1960) This famous actor was born in Cadiz, Ohio. He made 12 movies in just one year. He won an Academy Award for his work.

Paul Newman (1925–) Newman became an actor after a knee injury. He is from Cleveland, Ohio. He won an Academy Award. His other interests include car racing and food production.

David "Davy" Crockett (1786–1836) Crockett ran away from home to become a soldier. Later, he became a lawmaker. This native of Greeneville, Tennessee, died at the Alamo in Texas.

Georgia O'Keefe (1887–1986) O'Keefe was a painter. She studied at the Art Institute of Chicago. She pioneered abstract art in America. She was born in Sun Prairie, Wisconsin.

Frank Lloyd Wright (1867–1959) This famous architect was born in Richland Center, Wisconsin. He designed buildings and entire cities. Students still study his work today.

Samuel "Mark Twain" Clemens (1835–1910) Twain was born Samuel Clemens in Florida, Missouri. He became a famous writer. Many of his works take place near the Mississippi River.

Favorite Cities

Chicago

Chicago, Illinois, is the largest city in the Midwest. It is a port and transportation center on the shore of Lake Michigan. Workers built the first steel-framework sky-scraper in Chicago in 1884. Today,

▼ *Chicago sits on the shores of Lake Michigan.*

Chicago is home to the Sears Tower. The Sears Tower is the world's tallest building. Chicago's O'Hare Airport is the world's busiest.

Chicago grew from a group of huts. The railroad came to Chicago in 1850. This helped the city grow even more. The railroad also

helped businesses thrive. A fire nearly destroyed Chicago in 1871. Residents quickly rebuilt the city.

Chicago is a leading industrial city. *Factories* make many goods, including telephone and TV equipment and radios. The city's largest industry is making metals like iron and steel. Large *commodity* trading centers are here, too. These are the Chicago Mercantile Exchange, the Midwest Stock Exchange, and the Chicago Board of Trade.

Visitors enjoy the Art Institute of Chicago, the Field Museum of Natural History, and the Museum of Science and Industry.

Cleveland

Cleveland, Ohio, is in northeastern Ohio on Lake Erie. It is a major port on the St. Lawrence Seaway. This industrial city produces electrical machinery, metals, vehicles, and aircraft.

People around the nation admire the Cleveland Orchestra. The Cleveland Museum of Art and Cleveland Museum of Natural History are other popular attractions. The city has professional

football, baseball, basketball, and soccer teams.

Moses Cleaveland laid out the city in 1796. The city grew quickly after the Erie Canal opened in 1825. The canal helped people ship iron ore and coal to Cleveland. This way, the city could produce metals. In 1870, the city became home to Standard Oil Company.

In 1967, voters elected Carl B. Stokes mayor. He became the first black mayor of a major U.S. city.

Detroit

Detroit, Michigan, is the largest city in Michigan. People call Detroit the "Motor City." Detroit workers make 22 percent of the cars and trucks in the United States. The city also produces steel for other industries.

Detroit became an important Great Lakes port in 1959. That is when the St. Lawrence Seaway opened. Today, dozens of steamship lines operate out of Detroit. The ships carry materials around the world.

Detroit began in 1701 as a frontier trading post and fort. The British

▲ *Detroit, Michigan, is often called "Motor City" because of its car-making industry.*

took over Detroit during the *French and Indian War*. The city stayed in British hands from 1760 until 1794. Then, Britain gave the city to the United States. A fire destroyed Detroit in 1805. Like Chicago, citizens quickly rebuilt their city.

Detroit remains a major shipbuilding, shipping and industrial center. The automotive industry began here in the early 1900s.

Memphis

Memphis, Tennessee, is the largest city in Tennessee. It sits on the Mississippi River in southwest Tennessee. Memphis is the business center of the South. It is a major distribution hub.

Memphis is home to the Memphis Cotton Exchange. The Exchange is the largest spot cotton market in the world. Memphis factories make wood products, farm implements, and automobile parts.

Memphis has a rich cultural history. It is the birthplace of *blues* music. Nearby is Graceland. Elvis Presley used to live at Graceland. Memphis also has its own music recording center, ballet, symphony, and opera.

Memphis began as Fort Prudhomme in 1682. The British had control of Memphis from 1763 until 1797. In 1797, Britain gave the city to the United States.

In the Civil War, *Union* forces attacked Memphis from the river. The Union soldiers won the battle and took over the city. In the 1870s, Memphis residents suffered an epidemic of yellow fever.

Nashville

Nashville, Tennessee, is known as the home of country music. Opryland U.S.A. is located in Nashville. Opryland is home of the Grand Ole Opry. Nashville has the nation's second-largest recording industry. The city produces the largest volume of country-music records.

Nashville has many factories, too. The factories make many goods like chemicals, food products, and shoes. Many of the city's buildings are in the Greek style of architecture. This has given it the nickname "Athens of the South." Nashville is home to Vanderbilt University and Fisk University.

Nashville began in 1779 as Fort Nashborough. Leaders renamed it in 1784. Residents built a solid system of roads and railroads. This helped the city grow rapidly during the 19th century.

◀ *Nashville, Tennessee, is often thought of as the home of country music.*

St. Louis

St. Louis, Missouri, is called the gateway to the Midwest. The city sits on both sides of the Mississippi River. The east side is in Illinois. Seven bridges connect the east and west sides. Much of the city experienced flooding in 1993.

St. Louis is a major transportation hub. It is a leading industrial city. Factories produce soap, beer, chemicals, and electrical equipment. St. Louis also is an educational and cultural center.

Visitors enjoy the Jefferson National Expansion Memorial. This is the Gateway Arch. The Arch is 630 feet tall. Visitors also enjoy the St. Louis Art Museum and the St. Louis Science Center.

French fur trader Pierre Laclede founded the city in 1764. It became a focal point of river trade after the Louisiana Purchase. St. Louis was a popular port for steamboats. Later, many rail passengers came to the city.

Fast Facts

Arkansas

Population: 2.4 million
Area: 53,187 square miles
Capital: Little Rock
Industries: Agriculture, electrical goods, forestry, manufacturing, mining, poultry.
State Flower: Apple blossom
State Bird: Mockingbird
Statehood Date: June 15, 1836

Illinois

Population: 11.4 million
Area: 56,345 square miles
Capital: Springfield
Industries: Agriculture, chemicals, finance, insurance, manufacturing, printing.
State Flower: Native violet
State Bird: Cardinal
Statehood Date: December 3, 1818

Indiana

Population: 5.5 million
Area: 36,185 square miles
Capital: Indianapolis
Industries: Agriculture, machinery, manufacturing, metals.
State Flower: Peony
State Bird: Cardinal
Statehood Date: Dec. 11, 1816

Iowa

Population: 2.8 million
Area: 56,275 square miles
Capital: Des Moines
Industries: Agriculture, automobile parts, farm machinery, fertilizer, insurance, manufacturing, meat packing and processing.
State Flower: Wild rose
State Bird: Eastern goldfinch
Statehood Date: Dec. 28, 1846

Kentucky

Population: 3.7 million
Area: 40,410 square miles
Capital: Frankfort
Industries: Agriculture, coal mining, construction, manufacturing, textiles.
State Flower: Goldenrod
State Bird: Cardinal
Statehood Date: June 1, 1792

Michigan

Population: 9.3 million
Area: 58,527 square miles
Capital: Lansing
Industries: Agriculture, automobile manufacturing, mining.
State Flower: Apple blossom
State Bird: Robin
Statehood Date: January 26, 1837

Missouri

Population: 5.1 million
Area: 69,697 square miles
Capital: Jefferson City
Industries: Agriculture, aerospace, electronics, food products, manufacturing.
State Flower: Hawthorn
State Bird: Bluebird
Statehood Date: August 10, 1821

Ohio

Population: 10.8 million
Area: 41,300 square miles
Capital: Columbus
Industries: Agriculture, livestock, manufacturing.
State Flower: Scarlet carnation
State Bird: Cardinal
Statehood Date: March 1, 1803

Tennessee

Population: 4.9 million
Area: 42,144 square miles
Capital: Nashville
Industries: Chemicals, communications, construction, electronics, transportation.
State Flower: Iris
State Bird: Mockingbird
Statehood Date: June 1, 1796

Wisconsin

Population: 4.9 million
Area: 56,153 square miles
Capital: Madison
Industries: Agriculture, communications, manufacturing, milk and cheese production, paper and wood products, transportation.
State Flower: Wood violet
State Bird: Robin
Statehood Date: May 29, 1848

Suggestions For Further Reading

Kids Learn America by Patricia Gordon and Reed C. Snow, Williamsburg Publishing Co.

Children's Atlas of the United States, Rand McNally & Company.

All About Our 50 States by Margaret Ronan, Random House.

Midwest and Great Plains edited by Walter Havighurst, The Fideler Company.

Let's Discover the States: Eastern Great Lakes by Thomas G. Aylesworth and Virginia L. Aylesworth, Chelsea House Publishers.

Great Lakes and Great Ships by John Mitchell and Tom Woodruff, Suttons Bay Publications.

Chicago With Kids by Sheribel Rothenberg and Ellen Dick, Chicago Review Press.

Daniel Boone—Young Hunter and Tracker by Augusta Stevenson, Aladdin Books.

Glossary

Assassin
A person who kills another person.

Bauxite
An ore used to make aluminium.

Blues
A style of music. The songs often have sad lyrics.

Cholera
A disease that spreads easily from one person to another. Cholera often kills the people who have it.

Commodity
A product people trade. Commodities often are agricultural products.

Continental Climate
The type of climate found in the middle of large continents. This is usually in the Northern Hemisphere.

Desegregation
To stop people from being separated because of their race.

Factories
Places where people make products.

French and Indian War
A war in North America from 1754–1763. French soldiers and Native Americans fought against British soldiers.

Glacier
A mass of slowly moving ice.

Homestead Act
A law passed by Congress in 1862. It gave settlers 160 acres of land. The settler had to live on the land and farm it.

Louisiana Purchase
A large territory west of the Mississippi River. The United States bought the land from France in 1803.

Pelts
Animal skins.

Stalactite
A rock formation. It looks like an icicle. It usually hangs from the roof or wall of a cave.

Stalagmite
A rock formation. It looks like an upside-down icicle. It sticks up from the floor of a cave.

Tributary
A river that flows into another river.

Yellow Fever
A disease that spreads easily from person to person.

Union
Name given to the Northern states during the United States Civil War.

Index